Debby Huysmans Elk Island Construction Workers

…/… Moscow

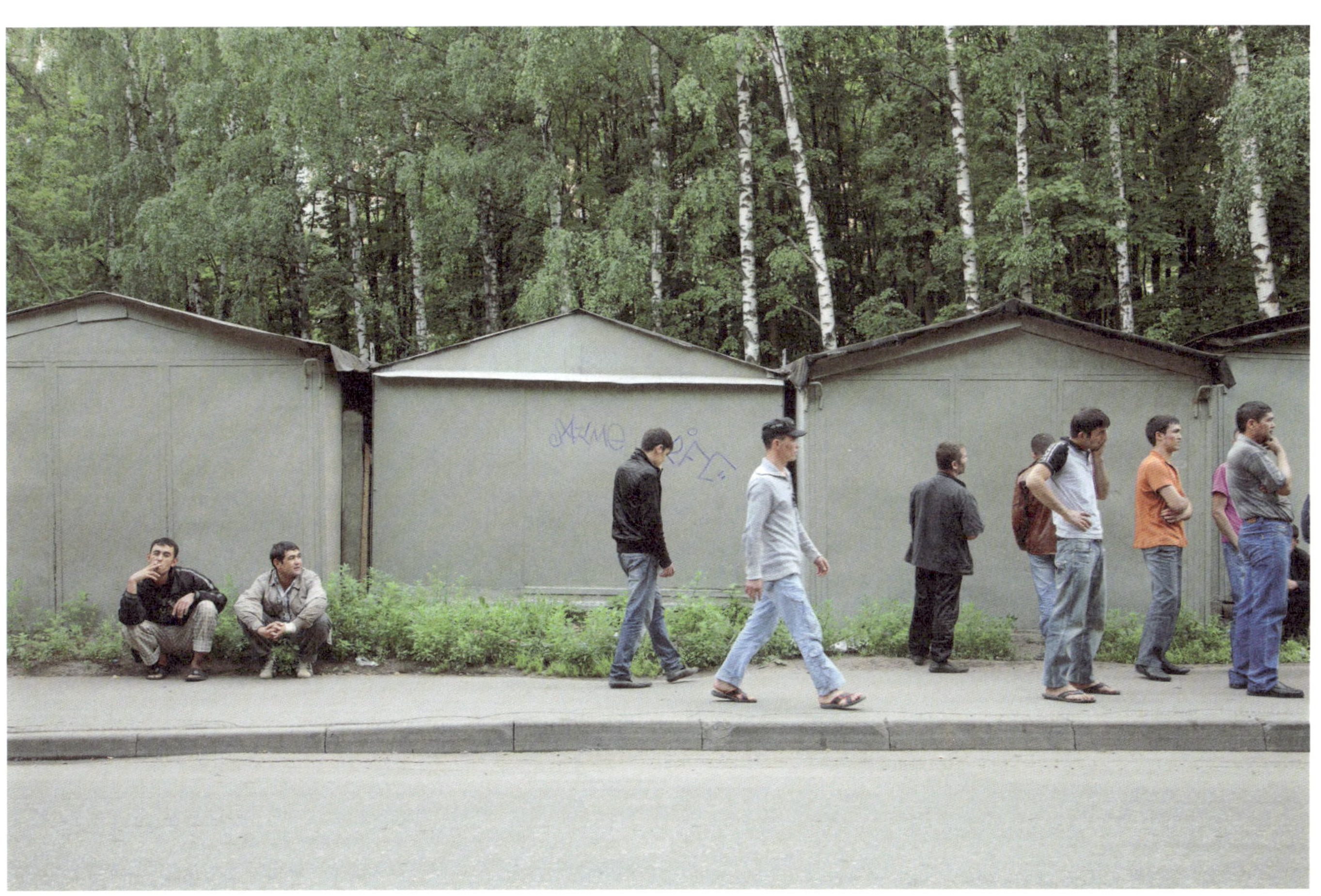

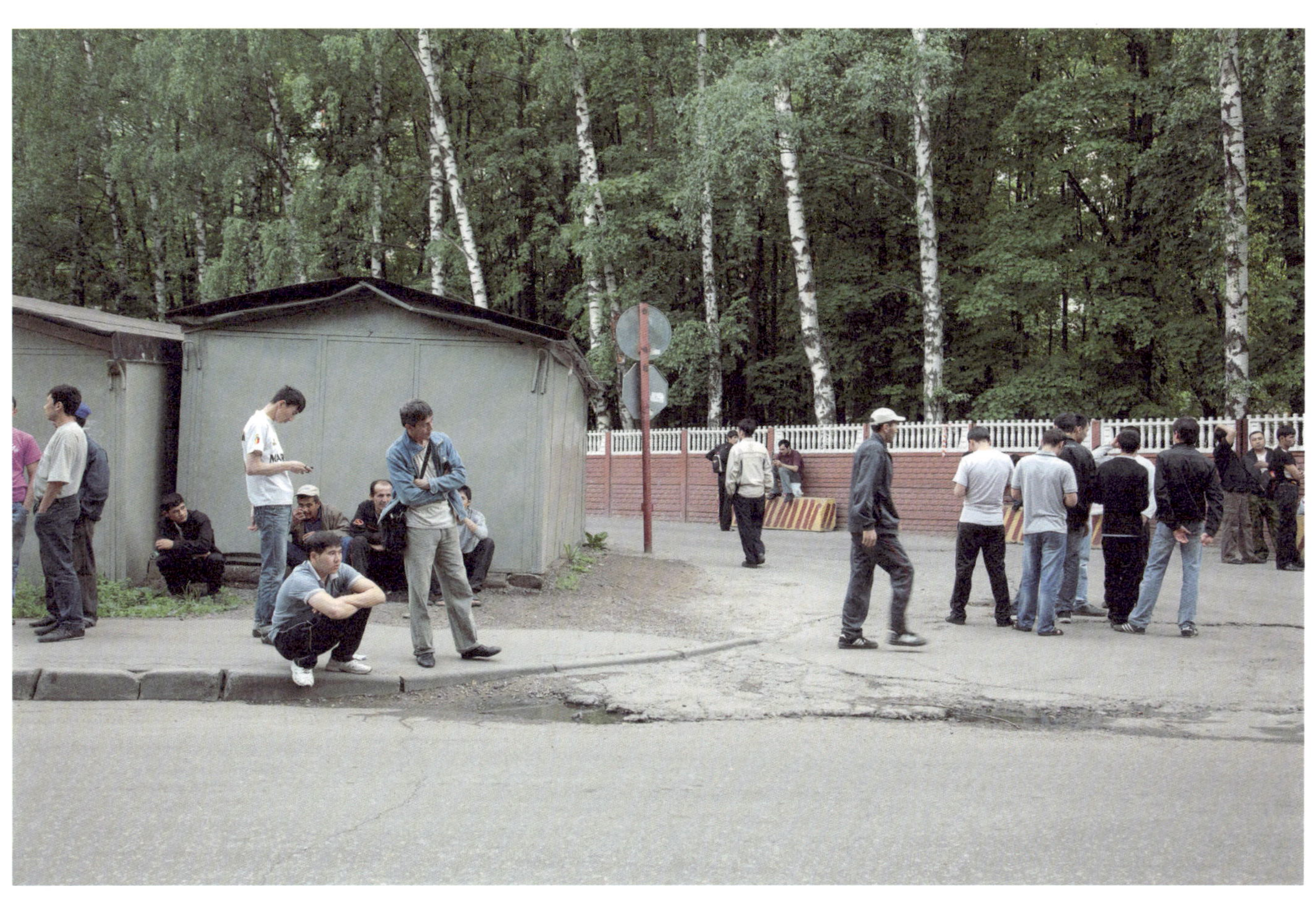

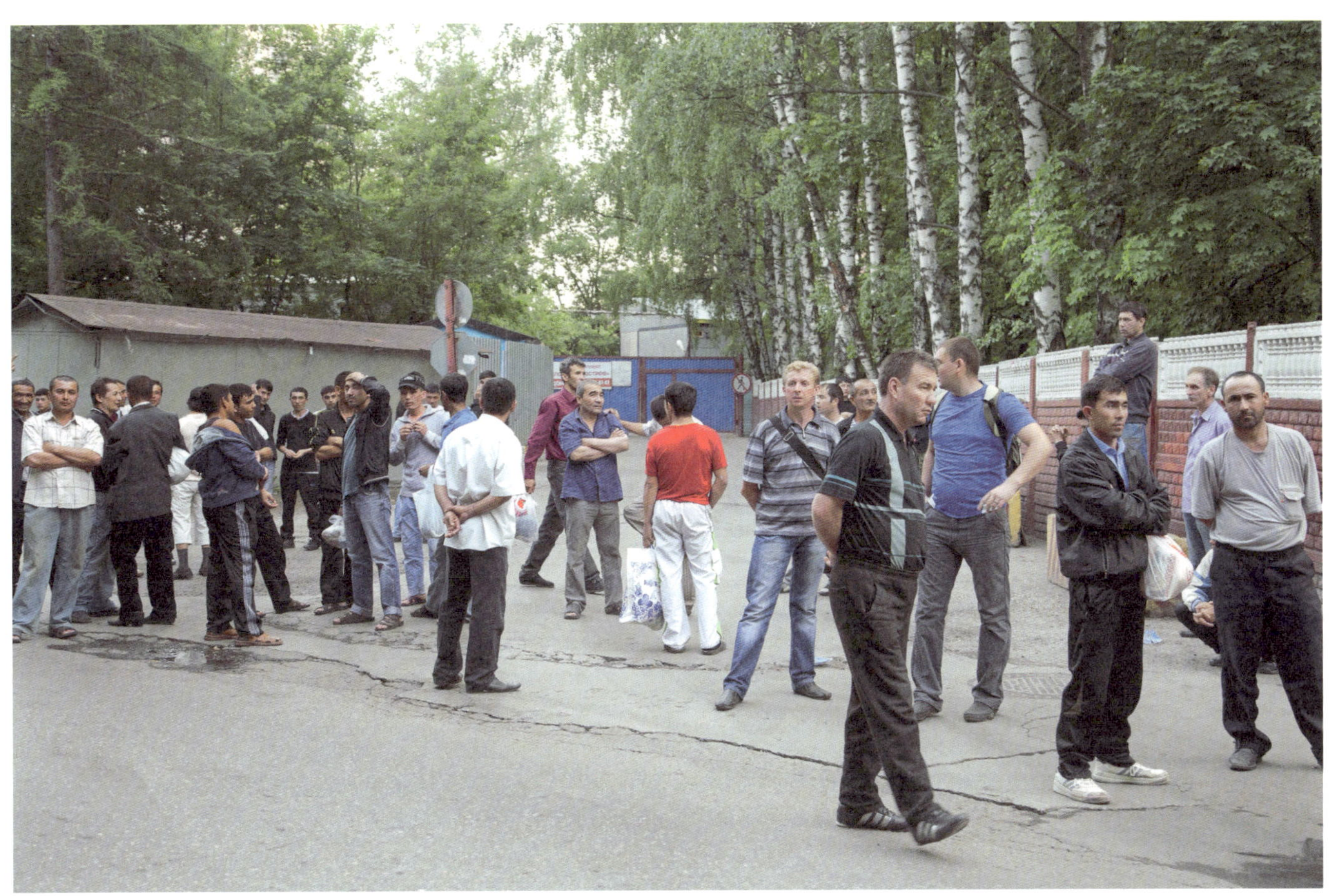

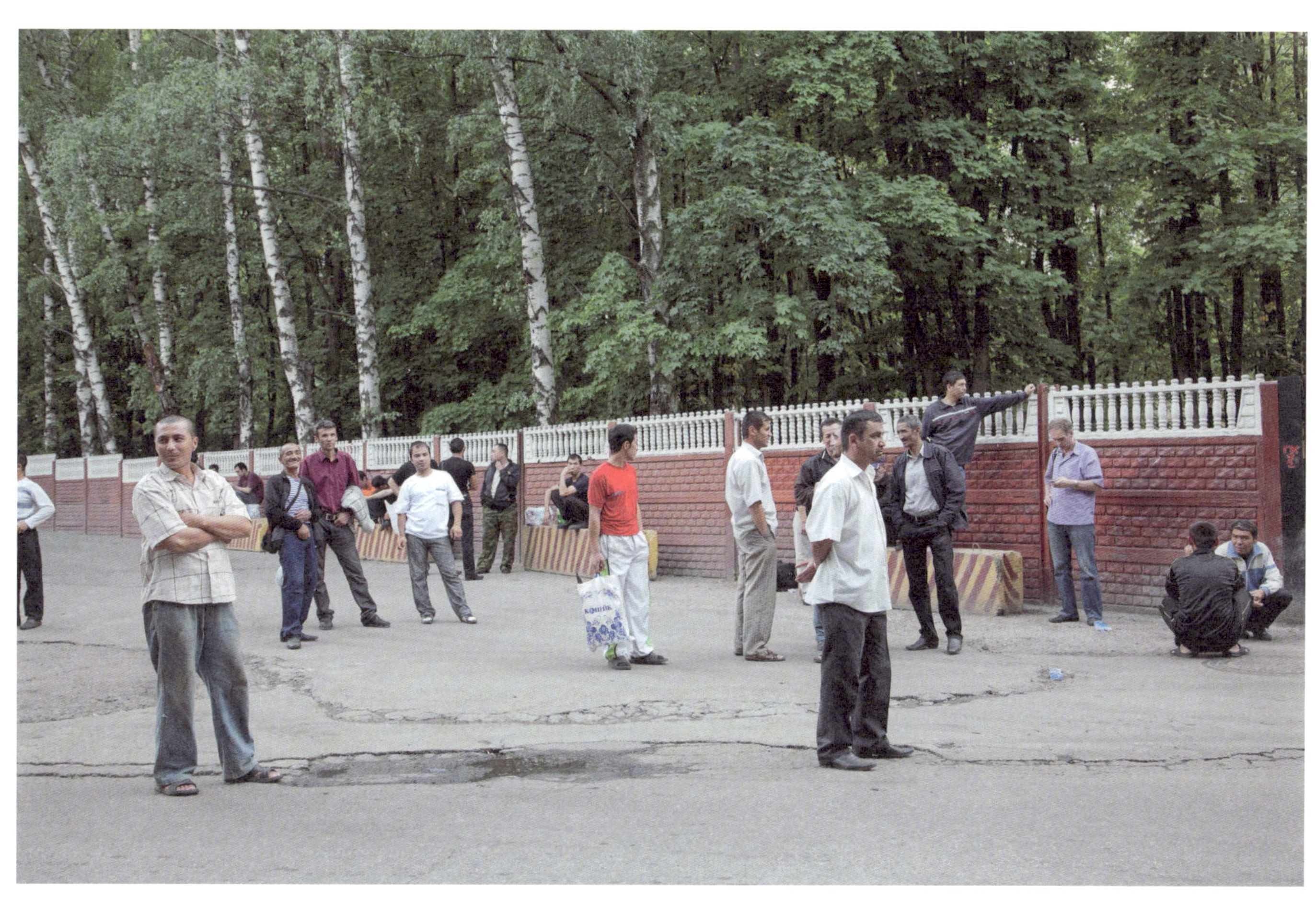

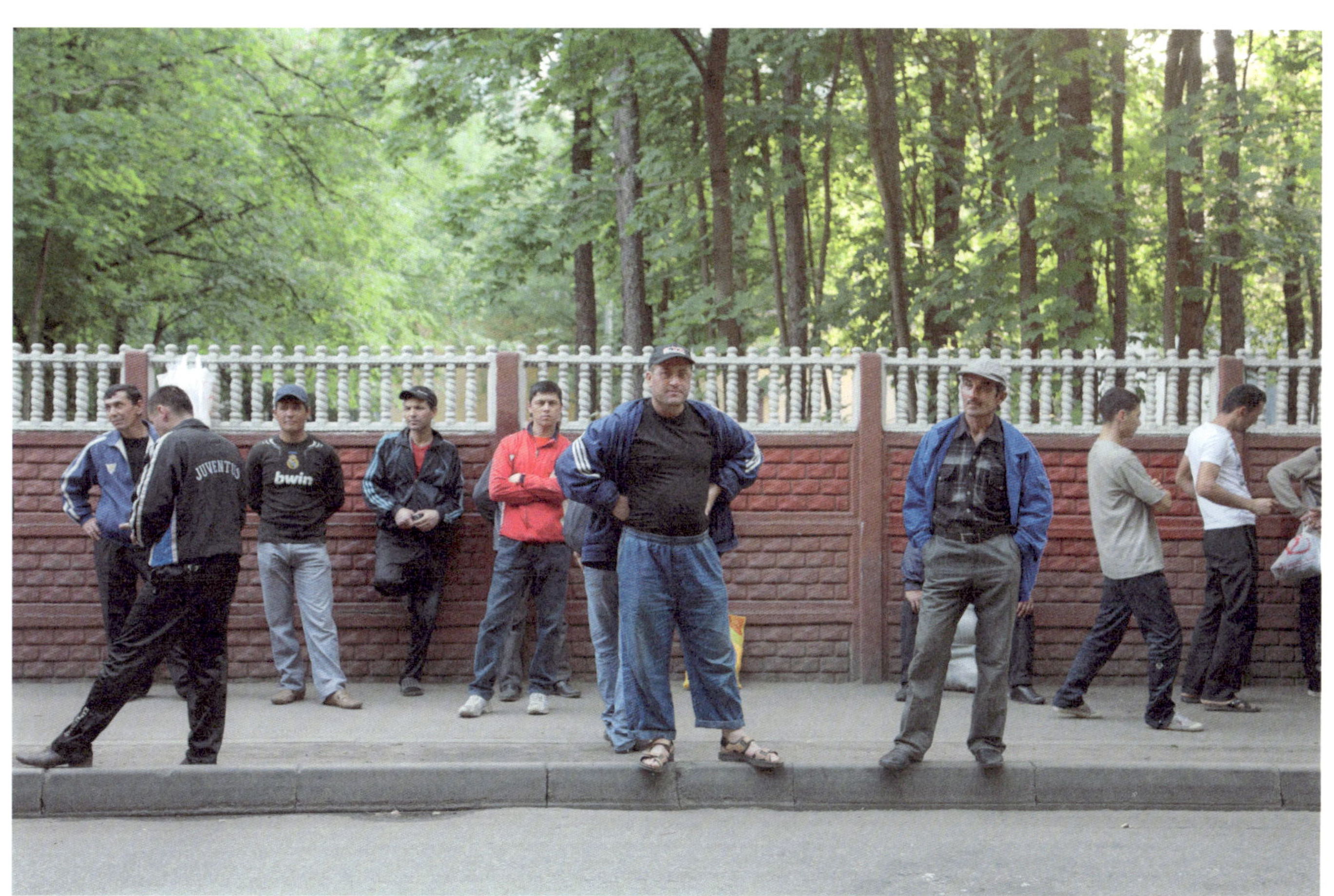
JUVENTUS
bwin

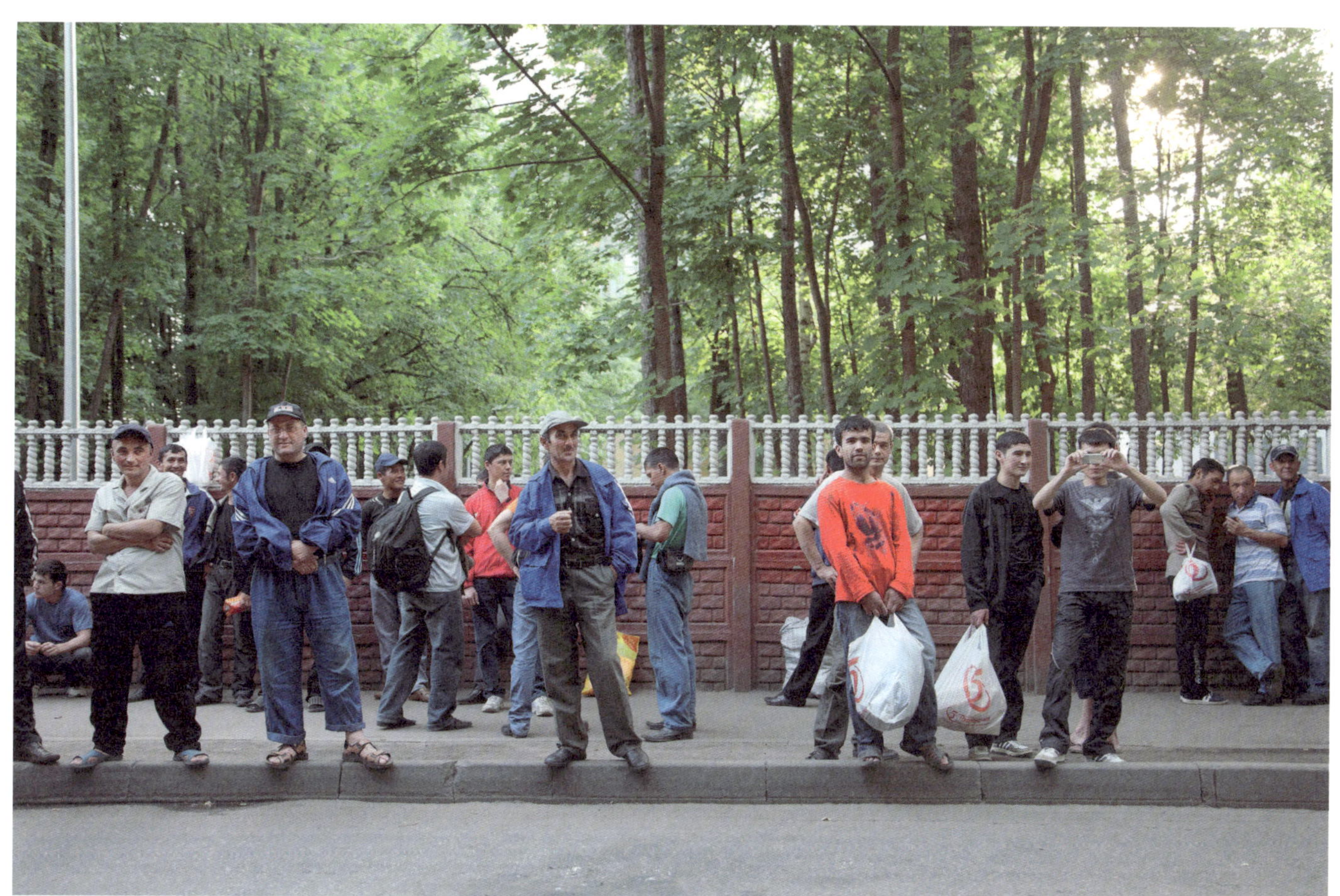

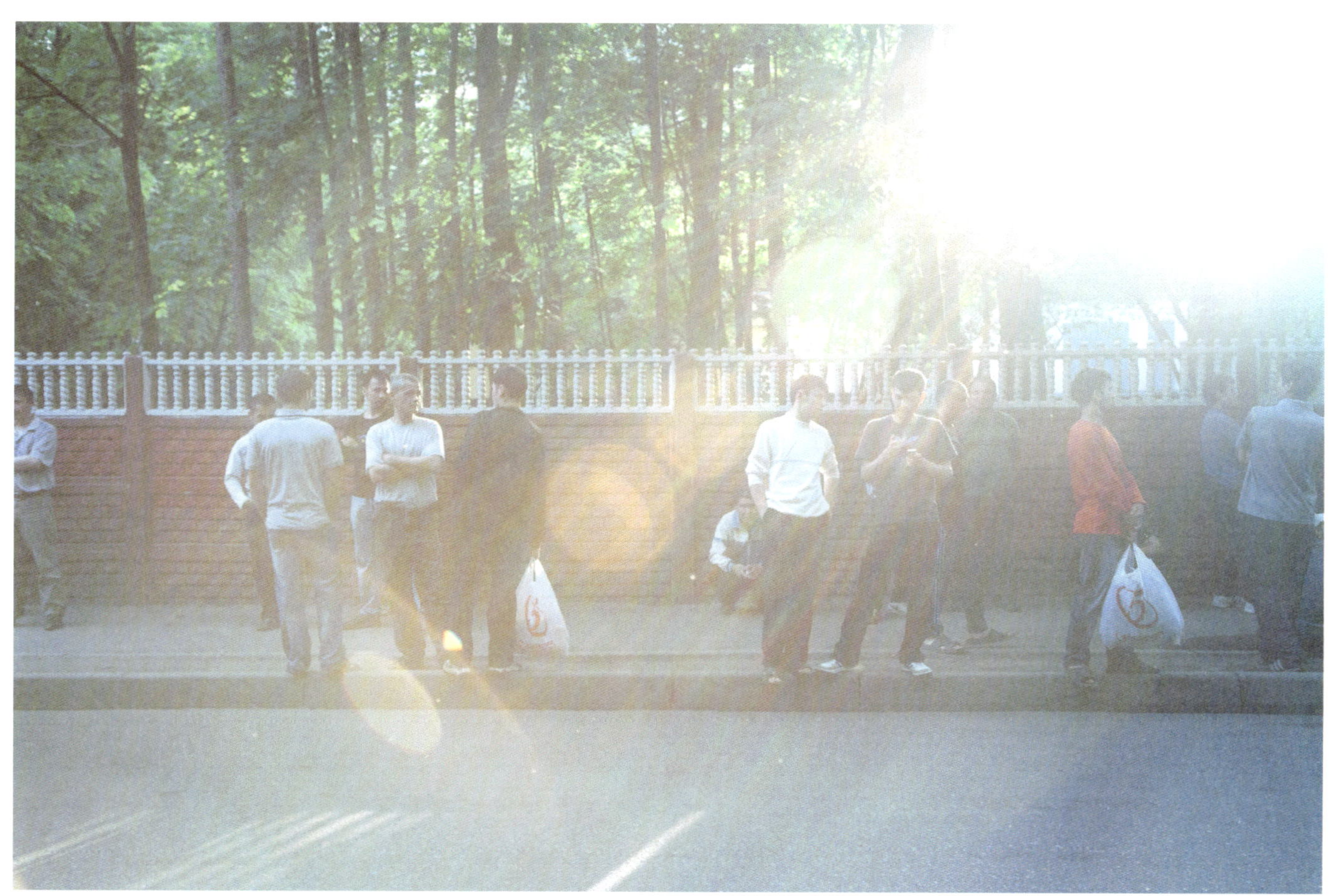

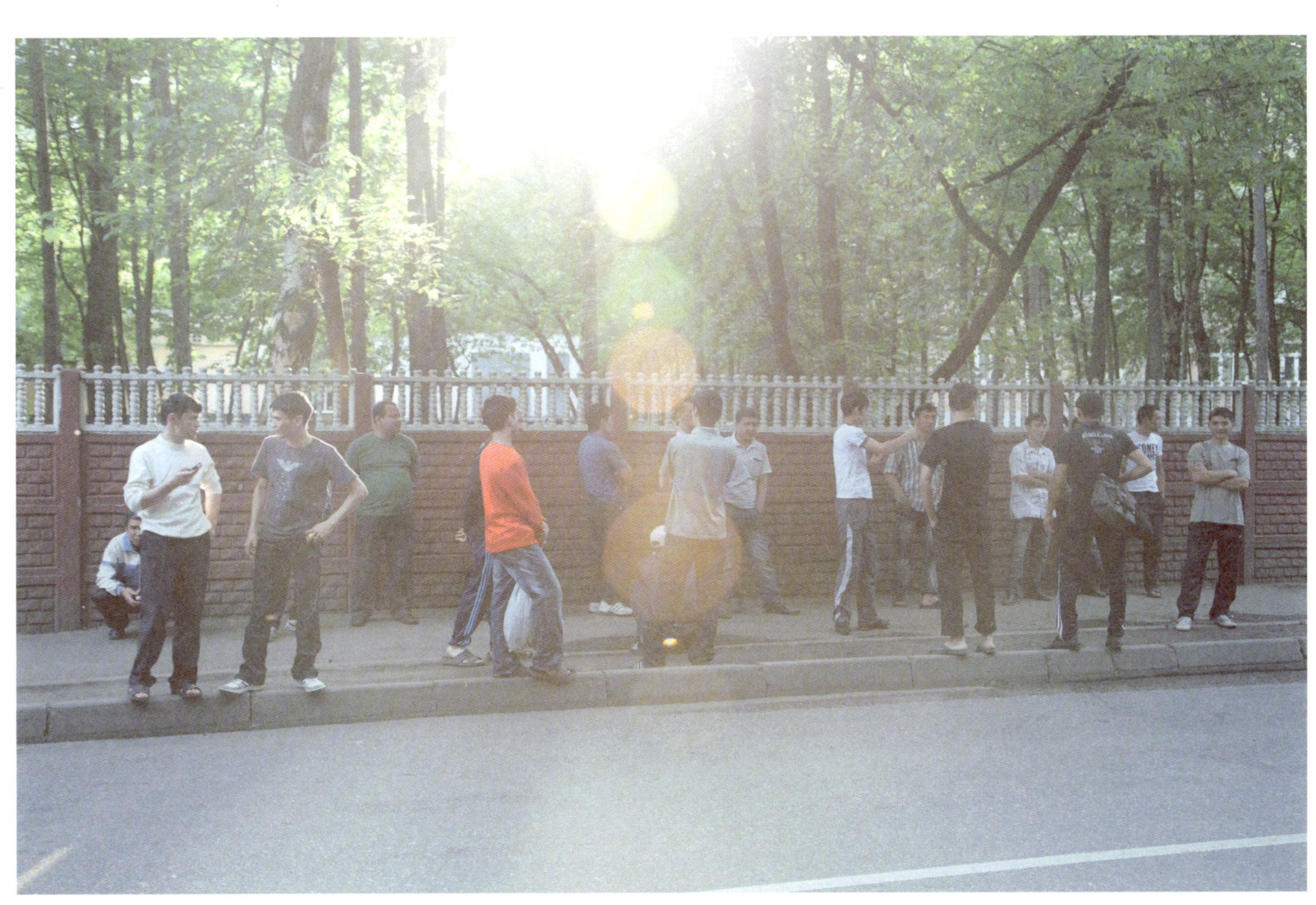

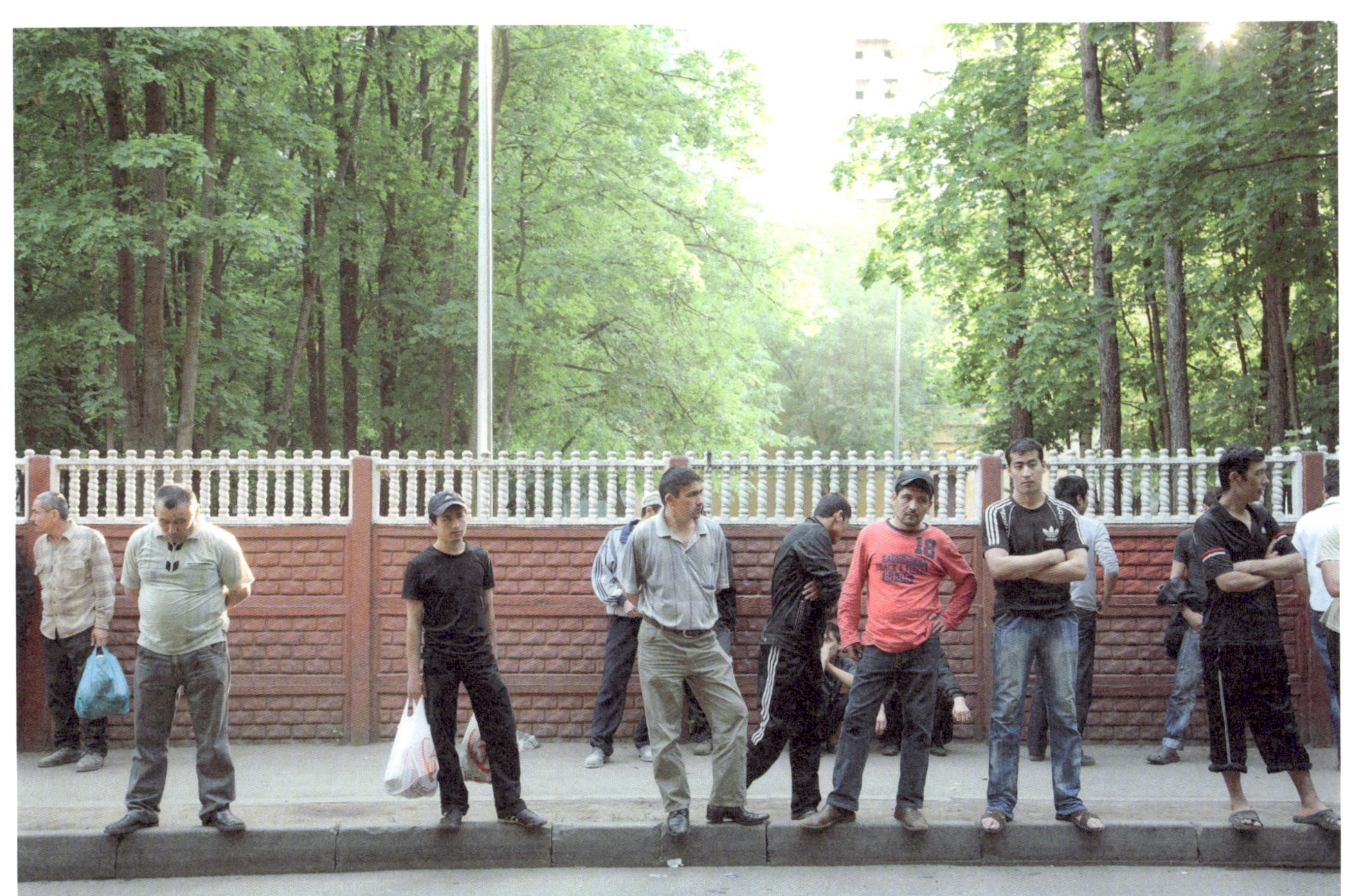
18

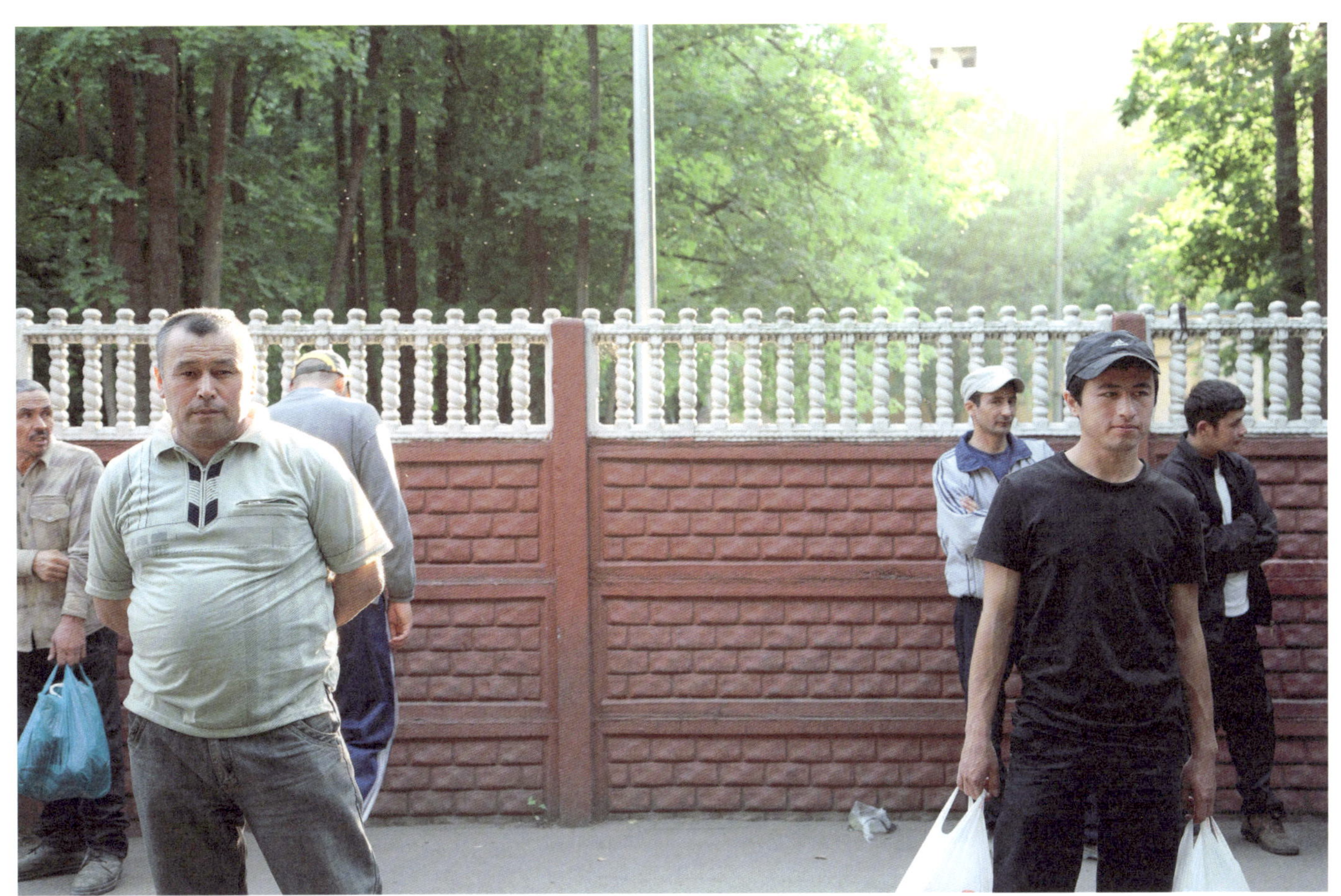

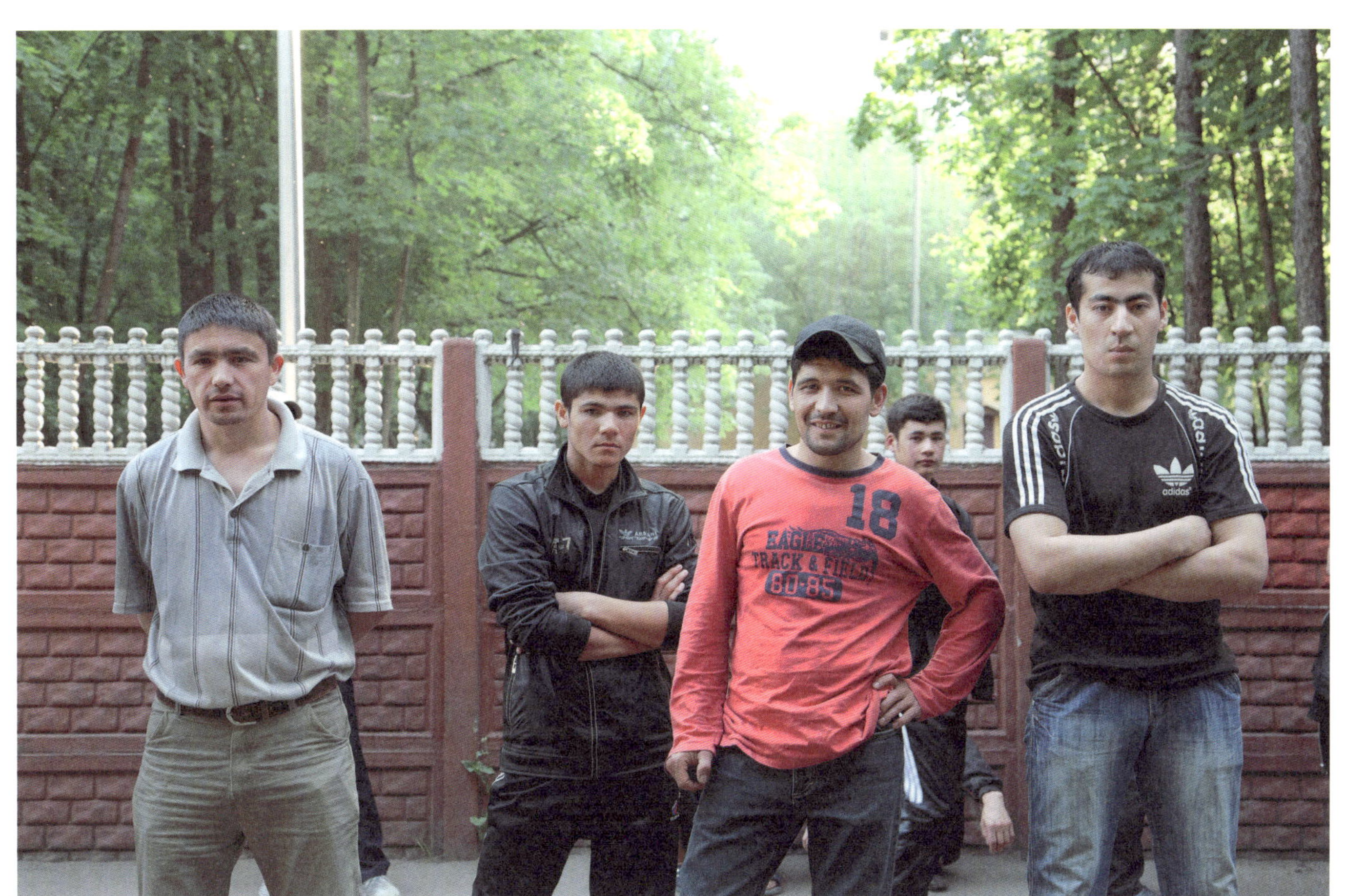
18
adidas

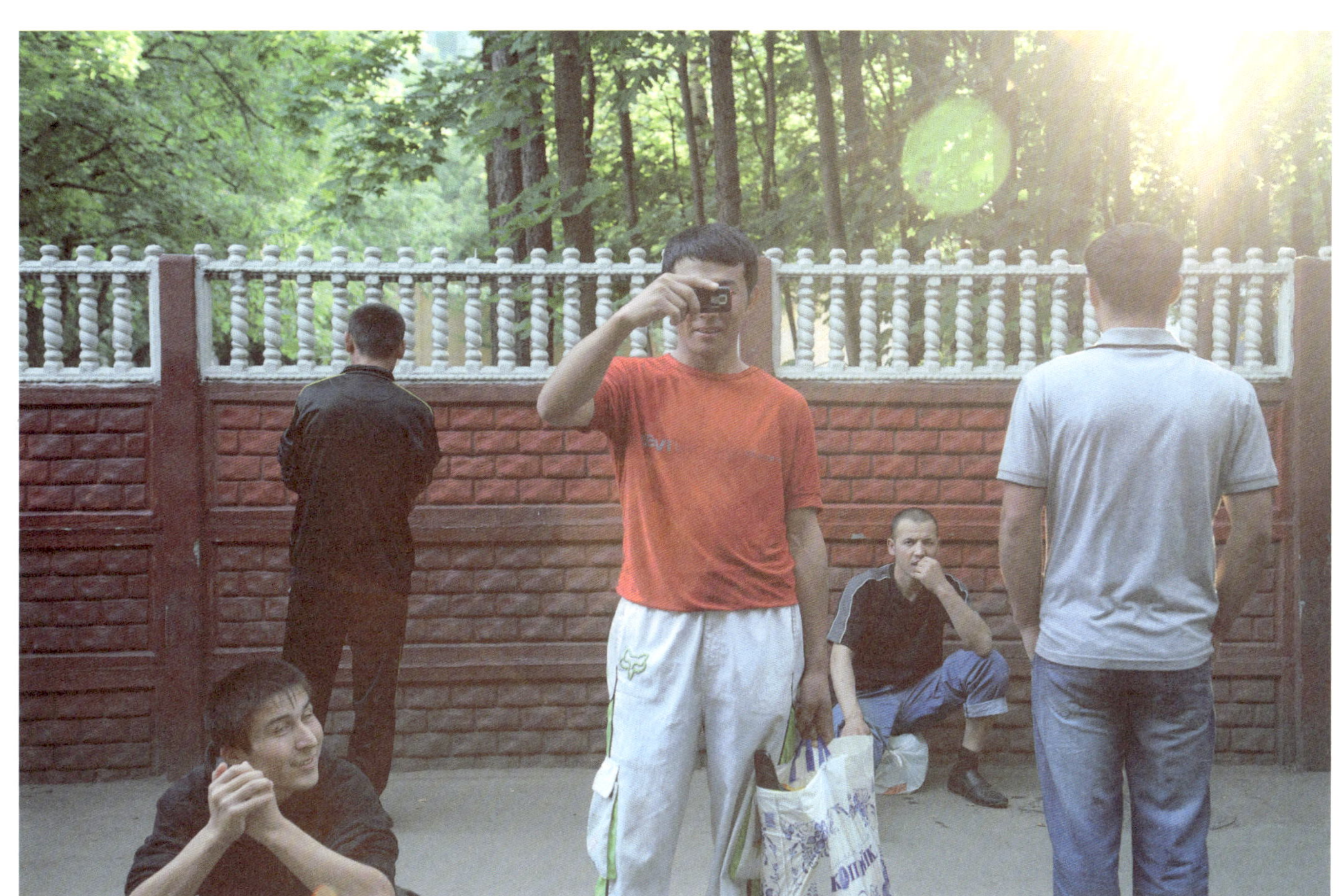

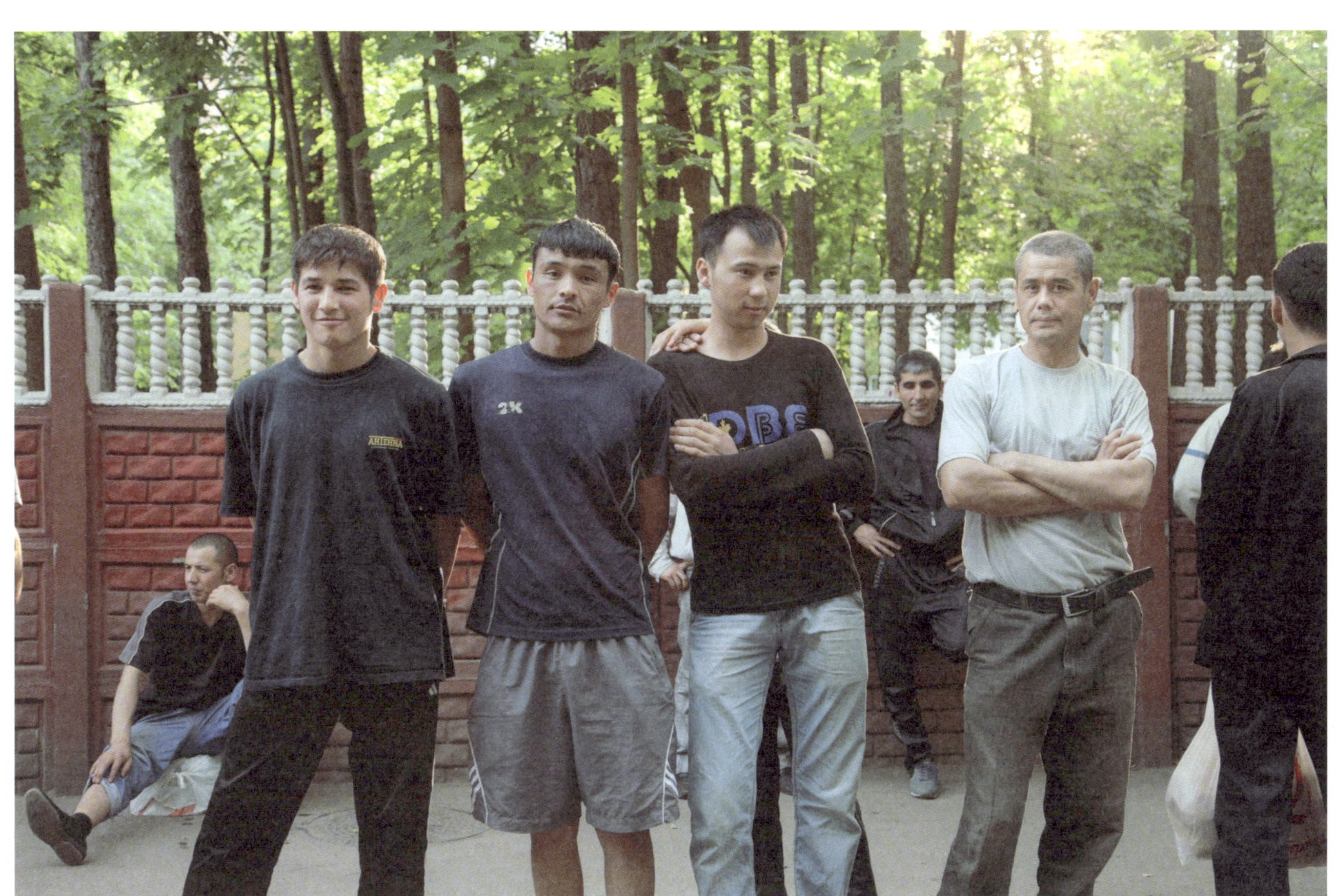

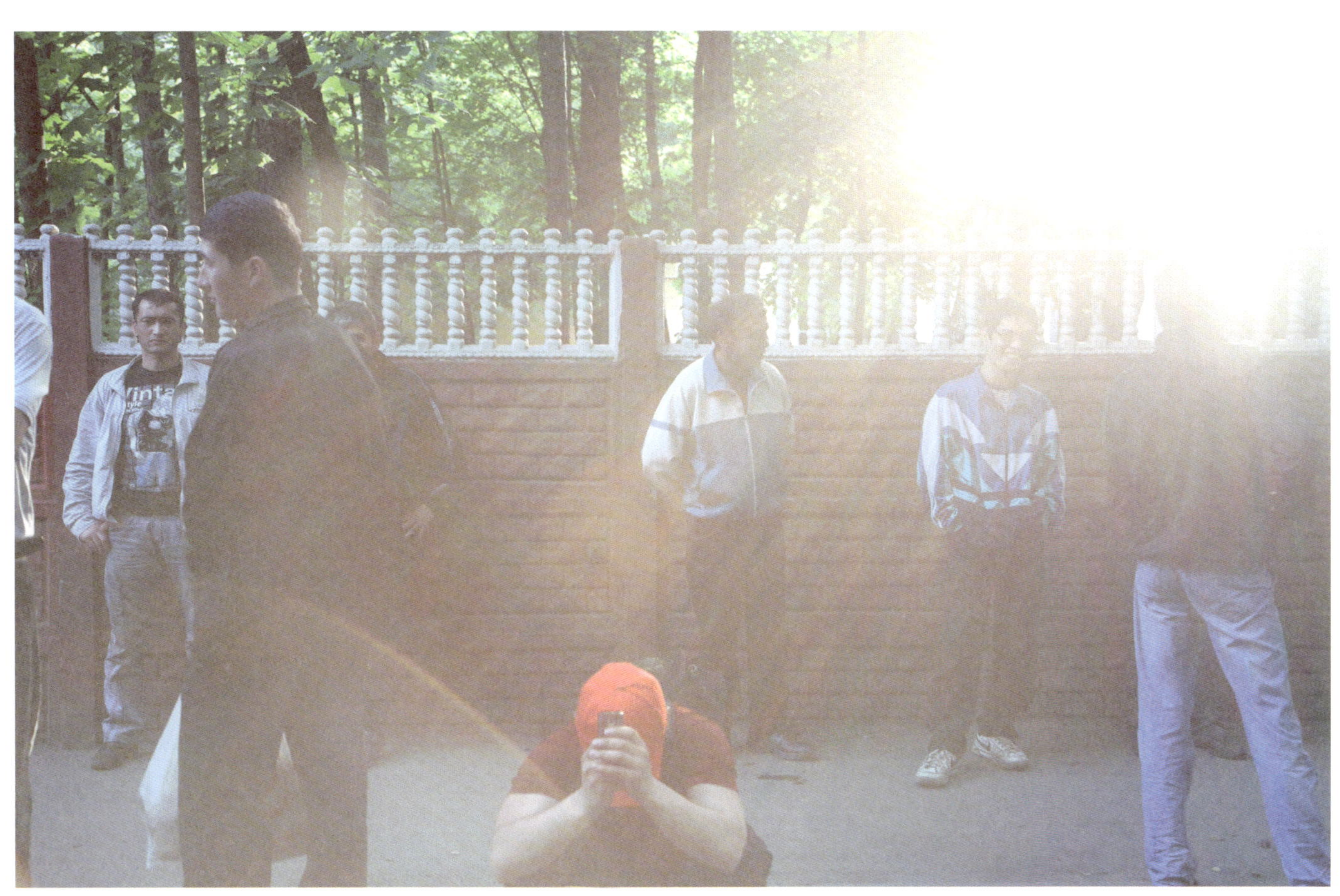

APE#061
Debby Huysmans
Elk Island Construction Workers Moscow

ISBN 9789490800413
www.artpapereditions.org
www.debbyhuysmans.be
First edition of 200 copies

Graphic design:
Studio Jurgen Maelfeyt
Printing: PurePrint, Oostkamp
Distribution: Idea Books, www.ideabooks.nl